SOD HOUSES ON THE GREAT PLAINS

Library of Congress Cataloging-in-Publication Data
Rounds, Glen, 1906–
Sod houses on the Great Plains / Glen Rounds.—1st ed.
p.   cm.
ISBN 0-8234-1162-1
1. Sod houses—Great Plains—Juvenile literature.   2. Frontier and
pioneer life—Great Plains—Juvenile literature.   [1. Sod houses.
2. Frontier and pioneer life—Great Plains.]
F596.R845   1995   94-27390   CIP   AC
693'.2—dc20
ISBN 0-8234-1263-6 (pbk.)

SOD HOUSES
ON THE GREAT PLAINS

written and illustrated by GLEN ROUNDS

Holiday House/New York

The first homesteaders to settle on the Great Plains—in what are now the states of Kansas, Nebraska, and the Dakotas—found good land there, but almost no trees suitable for building log cabins, as they'd done on other frontiers.

For temporary living quarters, they pitched tents or set their canvas-covered wagon boxes on the ground. But the violent Plains winds and thunderstorms made the flimsy shelters unsatisfactory.

It wasn't until they had started plowing their first
fields that they discovered that the long tough ribbons
of prairie sod their plows turned up could be chopped
into blocks and used as building material.

Before starting to build a sod house, the home-steaders drove stakes to mark the corners of the new building, then chopped a supply of the sod blocks and hauled them to the building site.

Laying the heavy blocks one on top of the other like oversized bricks, they built the walls to full height, leaving an opening for the door in front and a small window hole in either side wall.

For the roof they first laid a ridge pole, with one end resting on the middle of the front wall and the other on the back. Then smaller poles were laid close together from the ridge pole to the walls on either side and covered with a thick layer of hay and weeds.

When that was done, they hauled a load of dirt and spread a layer four to six inches deep on top of the hay, which was supposed to keep the dirt from sifting between the poles into the room below.

When the new sod house was ready for the family to move into, grass still grew on the floor. And until the settler could find lumber for a door, a piece of canvas or an old quilt could be hung over the opening, and paper rubbed with bacon grease let a little light through the window holes.

Most sod houses were small. Twelve by fourteen or sixteen by twenty feet square was the usual size, so living space was somewhat cramped, to say the least.

The cramped space wasn't the only disadvantage of living in a sod house.

For one thing, the dirt roofs tended to leak. Settlers claimed that after an hour's rain, water would drip inside for three days, making housekeeping difficult, what with puddles on the dirt floor and all.

Uninvited wildlife was another housekeeping problem. Field mice often burrowed into the sod walls and even nested in the hay on the roof. So, occasionally, a snake hunting mice overhead might fall between the ceiling poles and drop into the room below.

But, with all their disadvantages, the sod houses were cheap to build, and with dirt roofs and sod walls two feet thick, the settlers were in no danger of being "burned out" by the great grass fires that often swept the Plains.

Instead of building four walls up from level ground, some settlers dug back into a hillside to make a "dug-out," then had to build only a front wall of sod and a dirt roof.

These were easier to build, but there was always the chance that a horse or cow might walk onto the roof and break through.

It was possible to judge how long a sod house had stood from the height of the grass and sunflowers growing on the dirt roof. The older the house was, the more it came to look like some unusual kind of florist's shop.

A "soddie" might last four or five years, but by that time lumber was usually available for the building of a larger and more conventional house.

But some settlers simply put down wood floors, replaced the leaky dirt roof with one of boards and tar paper—sometimes even adding another sod-walled room or two—and continued to live in the old sod house for some years longer.